21ST
CENTURY
DEBATES

THE INTERNET

THE IMPACT ON OUR LIVES

IAN GRAHAM

A Harcourt Company

Austin New York
www.steck-vaughn.com

Published by Raintree Steck-Vaughn Publishers,
an imprint of Steck-Vaughn Company

Library of Congress Cataloging-in-Publication Data
Graham, Ian.
The internet: the impact on our lives / Ian Graham.
p. cm.—(21st century debates)
Includes bibliographical references and index.
ISBN 0-7398-3173-9
1. Internet—Juvenile literature. [1. Internet.] I. Title. II. Series.

ZA4201 .G68 2000
303.48'33—dc21 00-059121

Printed in Italy. Bound in the United States.
1 2 3 4 5 6 7 8 9 0 05 04 03 02 01

With thanks to Glen Raphael, and to Tina Naylor, PR Manager of Autodesk UK. Thanks also to those organizations who allowed us to use images from their web sites, including CyberGuards, Femail, Index on Censorship and Quackwatch. All screen shots in this book appear courtesy of the producers of the web sites they depict and remain the copyright of those producers. Every effort has been made to contact the copyright holders of the screen shots in this book. If any rights have been omitted the publishers apologize and will rectify this in any subsequent editions.

Picture acknowledgments: AFP/Corbis 8, 25, 50; Corbis 7 (Michael S. Yamashita), 21 (Liba Taylor), 23 (Owen Franken), 26 (Walter Hodges), 33 (Bojan Brecelj), 36 (Michael S Yamashita), 51 (Catherine Karnow); Digital Art/Corbis 10; Electrolux 54; Chris Fairclough 15; Ronald Grant Archive 39 (Mark Tillie/United Artists), 46; Panos Pictures 35 (Marcus Rose); Popperfoto 12, 16; Popperfoto/Reuters 18, 20, 24, 30, 34, 40, 41, 44, 45, 49, 55, 58; Reuters Newsmedia Inc./Corbis 47; Science Photo Library 5 (Mike Agliolo), 6 (David Parker), 11 (NCSA, University of Illinois), 13 (John Greim), 29 (David Parker), 56 (Will and Deni McIntyre), 59 (Mehau Kulyk); Tony Stone Images 17 (Hunter Freeman), 32 (P. Crowther/S. Carter), 43 (Bob Schatz), 52 (Mark Lewis); Tesco 9; Text 100/Microsoft 22.

Cover: foreground picture shows a girl using the Internet (Science Photo Library); background picture shows computer terminology (Pictor International Ltd).

CONTENTS

The Information Superhighway 4

Using the Internet 6

Freedom of Information 18

Growing Up with the Internet 24

E-business 32

Net Crime 38

Future Developments...52

Glossary 60

Books to Read 61

Useful Addresses 62

Index 63

THE INFORMATION SUPERHIGHWAY

FACT

The first computer-to-computer link-up was made in October 1969, when a computer at the University of California, Los Angeles (UCLA) was connected to a communications line with a second computer at the other end, at the Stanford Research Institute.

The Internet—Necessity or Luxury?

At the beginning of the twenty-first century, people have created the technology to send vast amounts of information to one another across thousands of miles instantly, at the touch of a button. What effects will this technology have on the lives we lead?

Technology changes society by changing what we do, how we do it, and, often, how quickly we can do it. The Internet, or Net, is already altering the way in which we work, play, and communicate with each other. And new ways of using it are being devised all the time.

VIEWPOINT

"I used to think that cyberspace was fifty years away. What I thought was fifty years away was only ten years away. And what I thought was ten years away was already here. I just wasn't aware of it."
Bruce Sterling, writer

Small beginnings

The computer network that became the Internet was invented in the 1960s to solve a problem in military research in the United States. The people who developed it never imagined that it would end up being used by hundreds of millions of people all over the world.

The Internet has undoubtedly yielded great benefits, but, like any new development, it also has its share of drawbacks. Criminals have seized on its potential for committing crimes in new ways. And law enforcement agencies have been slow to catch up with their activities. The rapid growth of the Internet also raises important questions about personal privacy, freedom of speech, and censorship. Some governments clearly feel threatened by the arrival of the Internet in their countries and are trying to control its use, or even ban it altogether.

FACT

The word Internet was used for the first time in 1982. The term "information superhighway" was popularized by the then U.S. Vice President Al Gore in 1993.

To censor, or not to censor?

While the Internet is international, the laws, beliefs, and moral standards that people live by vary enormously from country to country. Internet material that is perfectly legal and acceptable in one country may cause outrage—or may even be illegal—elsewhere. Some people argue that certain material should be blocked to safeguard moral standards and keep Internet content within the law. But other people argue with equal conviction that censorship of the Net is itself unacceptable because it restricts free speech and the free expression of ideas.

DEBATE

Should the Internet be controlled in the interests of national security, or for legal or moral reasons? Or should it be a free and open market place for the exchange of ideas and information?

The Internet began as a useful tool for scientists. Then it became possible for the general public to use it by linking a personal computer to a telephone line by means of a modem. At first the Internet was a luxury, mainly for computer enthusiasts, but now it is rapidly becoming a necessity for businesses and increasing numbers of ordinary people.

Whatever the rights and wrongs of the Internet, its recent growth has been impressive. Every month, fifteen million more people are connected to the Net, or "go on-line." This book will look at some of the issues raised by this amazing new global network.

The Internet links personal computers all over the world through the global public telephone network of cables and satellites.

USING THE INTERNET

A Free Market, or Risky Business?

Writers often predict new developments in technology before they actually happen. In his 1984 book *Neuromancer*, the writer William Gibson invented the word "cyberspace" to describe an imaginary world created by a computer. Gibson's cyberspace was a three-dimensional computer-generated world that looked, smelled, felt, and sounded real. Cyberspace is now used to mean the World Wide Web, a worldwide network of interlinked pages of information accessed using the Internet. Gibson's vision of cyberspace is what we now call virtual reality. This vision continues to influence designers who would like the Internet to feel more like a real environment, and less like pages of text.

A computer scientist updates pages on the World Wide Web at CERN, the European particle physics laboratory near Geneva, Switzerland.

On the Internet, a group of pages of information is called a web site. There are now about ten million web sites worldwide, containing a total of about one billion pages. Every web page is linked to other pages by hyperlinks. Clicking on a link takes you straight to the new page.

Anything that involves the exchange of information between people can be done on-line. You can now buy, sell, communicate, use an Internet bank, teach, learn, and work from home. On-line stores sell everything from CDs, books, and videos to cars, boats, and even houses. The first on-line shoppers had limited demands. They were computer enthusiasts and "gadget freaks," most of whom were young men. But as a wider range of people went on-line, businesses saw the opportunity to market a greater diversity of products and services.

Working the Net

For anyone who deals mainly with information, the Internet makes it possible to work from almost anywhere. Using a portable computer connected to the Internet by mobile phone, it is possible to work and keep in touch with the rest of the world just as easily at home, on a park bench, or on the beach as it is in a conventional office. Growing numbers of people are working at home instead of commuting to and from the office on crowded roads and railroads. However, not everyone is likely to be allowed the chance to work from home. And those who are may find that they miss the contact with other people at work.

People who have traditionally worked away from base are using the Internet too. Journalists, for example, used to have to file their stories with their newspapers by dictating them over the phone, but now they can keystroke a story into a portable

FACT

The World Wide Web, or "Web," was created by Tim Berners-Lee and his colleagues at the European nuclear science research center, CERN, in Switzerland. They wanted to find a way for researchers to share their work and link related thoughts together. Work on the Web started in 1989 and it was released to the public in 1992.

A scientist in the field files a report by e-mail, using a satellite antenna to link her personal computer to the Internet.

computer and send it straight into the newspaper's computer system by electronic mail (e-mail).

Shopping and banking

Any product or service that can be ordered by phone or mail and almost any routine banking service can be dealt with on-line. There are thousands of on-line stores already and more banks are going on-line every day. But many people are reluctant to send out private details such as credit card numbers or bank account numbers via the Net for fear that someone else could pick them up and use them illegally. The public perception that shopping on-line may not be safe is a major obstacle to rapid growth. A survey carried out by the credit card organization Visa found that only five percent of consumers across the European Union feel safe spending money via the Internet.

On-line shopping saves time and shoe-leather by bringing the merchandise to your computer screen.

Despite people's distrust, on-line shopping is steadily growing as people try it out. More than three-quarters of all on-line shopping purchases are computer software and hardware and books, with travel, music, and clothing lagging some way behind. At the moment, most shoppers want to go to stores and look at products before buying them. But we may not always feel that way.

If it is possible to order clothes on-line, why bother going to clothing stores? If it's cheap and easy to transfer, or "download," music and movies from the Web, why bother buying disks, tapes, and videos from stores? If you can order your food and general household supplies on-line, why spend time wheeling a heavy shopping cart around a supermarket? Anything that affects the way people shop also affects the way our towns look. When supermarkets drew people out of city centers to giant out-of-town complexes, local grocers, butchers, and bakeries disappeared. We still have these services in every town, but in a fraction of the numbers that used to exist.

If the shift to on-line shopping continues or even accelerates, it, too, could affect the numbers and type of stores in our streets in a similar way. Alternatively, if our main street stores all go on-line, then they may find their sales rising as they attract shoppers from the rest of the world. They may become centers for supplying goods by mail order and also have a few walk-in customers. More shoppers staying at home and buying on-line should mean fewer cars on the roads. But, since all the goods ordered on-line have to be delivered, the number of delivery vehicles will probably increase.

Auction houses are very eager to get on-line. An auction room might hold a couple of hundred people and serve a handful of telephone bidders. But an on-line auction house can attract buyers from all over the world. More buyers may result in more competitive bidding, which should push prices up and earn higher commissions for the auction houses.

As more of the retail stores and businesses we deal with open web sites, it becomes difficult to assess how good or bad they are and whether or not to trust them. Should we be able to check out businesses on the Web with an impartial agency before we risk spending our money with them? If

VIEWPOINTS

"There is no evidence that the Internet will replace the traditional shopping cart and plastic-bag trip."
Edward Heathcoat Amery, political analyst and journalist

"[Our findings demonstrate] a growing confidence in the use of the Internet for shopping as an increasing proportion of users become more familiar and comfortable with the process of undertaking on-line transactions."
From a UK National Opinion Polls survey on Internet shopping

Many supermarkets are now on-line and deliver goods ordered via the Internet.

the agency is free to customers and financed by the businesses, would it really be reliable and impartial?

E-mail brings an electronic mailbox within the reach of any computer.

Internet shoppers are often people who are too busy to shop in the usual way. But most deliveries are made during the day when people are at work. In the future, there will be a growing need for evening deliveries. At the moment Internet businesses are mostly low-staff, low-cost enterprises, but so many new ones are starting up that they will become increasingly important job providers.

E-mail

Using electronic mail, or e-mail, anyone with a computer connected to the Net can send messages to anyone else with a computer connected to the Net. E-mail has transformed the way we communicate. It enables people to contact each other and respond to messages within minutes. Unlike a telephone conversation, which leaves no printed record, an e-mail message can be printed out. Businesses are now using printouts of e-mails as records of discussions, agreements, and actions.

If millions of e-mails are being sent every day, the postal service must be losing a lot of business. Well, no, actually. The number of letters and packages being sent is still increasing—and e-mail is contributing to this increase. The growth of on-line shopping has produced a measurable increase in package deliveries—up to ten percent during the 1999 Christmas season in some countries.

FACT

The country with the highest percentage of its population on-line in 1999 was—the United States? Japan? No, it was Iceland (forty-five percent).

E-mail is normally released from a mailbox to a computer that can provide the right user name and password. Both of these are stored in the computer when an Internet service account is set up. Internet Service Providers (ISPs) are companies that offer connections to the Internet. Picking up your e-mail usually means making a local call to the ISP that hosts your mailbox. Picking up your e-mail when you are traveling around is trickier. Travelers can use a different type of e-mail, called webmail, that is easier to use from different computers and places. A webmail service is located at a web site. Anyone setting up a webmail account can pick up e-mails simply by logging onto the web site and key stroking in the necessary security and identification information, so it doesn't matter which computer is used.

Although e-mail is great for contacting people far away very quickly, it is often used to contact people on the other side of the same office or to send messages that could be dealt with better by a phone call. So could e-mail be making us lazy and discouraging us from having face-to-face contact with each other?

In the short term, the social effects are not particularly marked. The same people who are e-mailing colleagues sitting nearby are also chatting with each other at lunchtime, talking to

FACT

A "host" is a computer system that provides Internet services. Scandinavia has more Internet hosts per head of population than anywhere else in the world, including the United States. Finland has about 120 hosts per 1,000 people, a fraction ahead of the United States. Iceland has about 100; Sweden, Canada, and Norway about 90; and Denmark 75. In the rest of Europe, the leaders are Switzerland and the Netherlands, both with about 55.

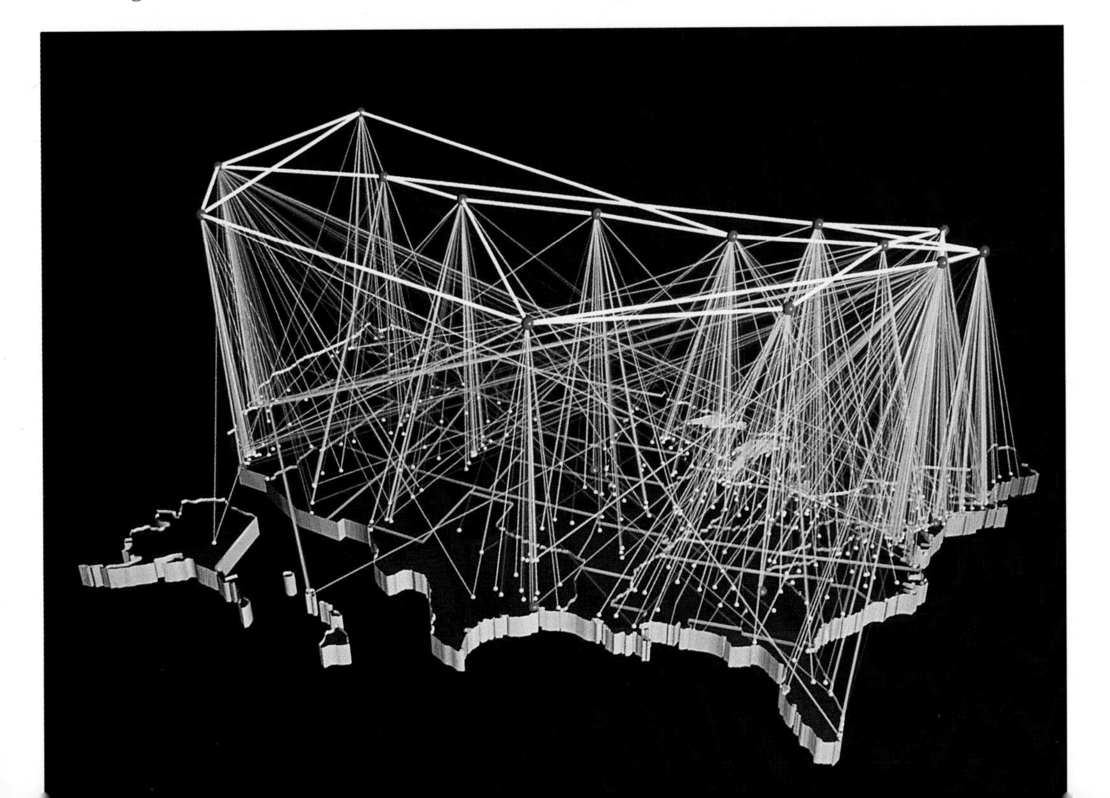

Data flows between computers in a U.S. national computer network. The colors represent traffic volume, from lowest (purple) to highest (white).

VIEWPOINTS

"The Net is a real waste of time, and that's exactly what's right about it."
William Gibson, writer

"It is lack of time that is driving women in droves to the Internet —the newest time-saving household appliance."
From **What Makes Women Click?** *by Gina Garrubo, Executive Vice President of Women.com Networks*

neighbors over the garden fence, visiting stores, and calling friends and relatives. But farther in the future, if we are all on-line, digital communication could replace this routine, daily face-to-face contact with people. And that might have undesirable consequences. When we communicate with other people, we don't rely on words alone. We also use a lot of nonverbal communication—we "read" people's facial expressions and body language and we listen to the tone of their voices. E-mail eliminates all of these nonverbal cues. But in the future we will have video-conferencing and one-to-one conversations using webcams (small video cameras used to send images across the Internet) that could ultimately replace the phone.

Of course, one communications medium we've been using all our lives—the telephone—is also incapable of communicating facial expressions or body language: and a lifetime of communication by telephone doesn't seem to have damaged us in any way. While it fails to transmit some of the non-verbal cues we use face-to-face, it has caused an explosive growth in communication because it enables us to contact more people over greater distances than was possible before. In the same

A young woman goes on-line in the first Internet café in the Iranian capital, Tehran, in 1998.

way, perhaps our fears about the implications of on-line communication will turn out to be groundless. One could argue that on-line shopping, banking, mail, and so on take much less time than traveling to stores, banks, and post offices in person, which leaves us more time for leisure or work, where we will meet each other in the "traditional" way.

FACT

In Saudi Arabia, there are twenty-six Internet Service Providers who offer Internet access services specifically for women.

Women on-line

There are so many people on-line now that distinct groups of Internet users are appearing. And companies selling products and services are beginning to target these groups. The fastest-growing group of people going on-line now is women. By the year 2000, almost half of all Intenet users were female, mostly busy career women. Women often have to combine work with running a home and bringing up a family. Their time is precious. They use the Internet's twenty-four-hour on-line shopping, banking, e-mail, advice, and research facilities to save time. Women are flocking on to the Internet in such numbers that they are an increasingly important group of customers. There are now ISPs providing services specifically for women.

Senior citizens go on-line to keep in touch with family members and to search for useful information.

More specialist web sites and ISPs will emerge to serve the needs of other special interest groups. In the United States, senior citizens control more than three-fourths of American wealth. However, they are often discriminated against because of age or disability. ISPs aimed specifically at older people are beginning to spring up. Once senior citizens learn how to use it, they spend as much time on the Net as young people. They often use it to keep in touch by e-mail with grandchildren and other relatives in faraway places.

FACT

If you were to read every page of every web site on the Internet, it would take at least six hundred years!

Fact or fiction?

The amount of information on the Net can be daunting, but its accuracy is sometimes a more serious concern. Whatever you want to know, no matter how obscure, the answer will be stored in a computer somewhere in the world. And programs called search engines will help you find it. Just visit a search engine web site, keystroke in your question, and the search engine will lead you to the web sites that hold the answers. But how do you know that the answers are correct?

Health and medical information is widely available on the Web. Much of it is accurate and reliable, but lots of it is not, so caution is necessary.

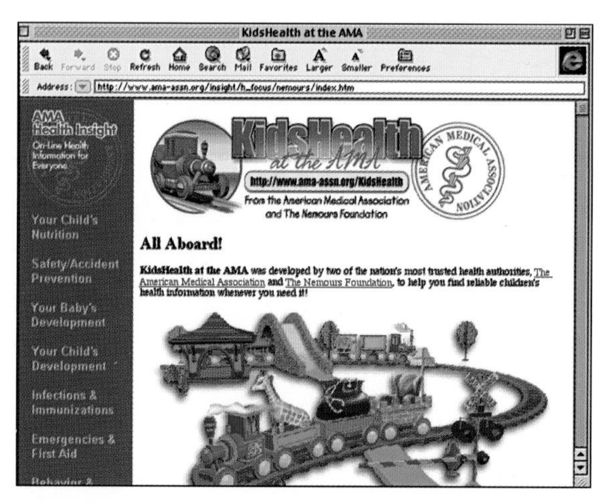

Anyone can set up a web site and air his or her beliefs on it, however strange these might be. Web sites stating that there are little green men living on the far side of the moon, or that the earth is flat, rarely do any harm because their claims are so outlandish. But web sites that claim to have a cure for cancer or AIDS can be dangerous. Doctors are concerned about bogus or misguided medical advice on the Web. It may be difficult to tell from a web site whether or not the advice it offers is based on science or simply reflects a desire to sell worthless treatments.

Hypochondriacs (people who are abnormally concerned about their health) can now check out the thousands of medical web sites and health stories on the Web. People who use the Internet to take health concerns to these absurd lengths are nicknamed cyberchondriacs. At the mercy of the Internet (rather than the respectable medical textbooks that hypochondriacs may pore over), cyberchondriacs can fall prey to the wildest claims made in the strangest web sites. Many of these are unknown to health and medical professionals and therefore go unchecked and unchallenged. On the plus side, however, there are web sites run by pharmaceutical companies at which you can put in your ailments and the company will recommend the drugs you should ask your doctor to prescribe. (But they will probably recommend only the drugs that they manufacture, of course!) The National Institute of Health (www.nih.gov) provides impartial health service information on-line.

With the help of a camera linked to the Web, parents at work can see what their children are doing at nursery school.

Webcams

You can use webcams to check out vacation resorts and look at street scenes in a town you're thinking of moving to. A handful of nursery schools and pre-school playgroups have installed webcams, so that working parents can access the cameras via the Web and see their children during the working day. There are built-in security measures so that only the children's parents can see the images.

Only time will tell if the use of webcams in schools and playgroups is a good idea, whether they help or harm parents' relationship with their children and whether they will be welcomed by teachers. Once webcams are placed in schools, they could be used for reasons other than parental monitoring. For example, if principals and school inspectors had access to classroom webcam images, perhaps the quality of teacher assessments and school

FACT

In 1993, three million people were using the Internet. By 1998, only five years later, that number had grown to 130 million. By the year 2000, that had grown to about one billion people on-line.

VIEWPOINTS

"The Internet has made it possible to have a memorial for all to visit. Perhaps to leave a dedication, or to take a moment and examine our own mortality."
From the web site of Golden Memorials

"Death is a very real thing—it's not virtual."
A Church of England spokesperson

inspections could be improved. But perhaps they could be used for less constructive reasons. Governments would be able to monitor teachers and control the way they teach certain subjects. Would the constant monitoring of any profession be desirable? Webcams are so small that they can be hidden anywhere. If a webcam can be placed almost anywhere, can any of us be sure that one isn't watching us right now? How would it feel to discover a webcam in one's room at home, or in your classroom? Perhaps the use of webcams should be controlled? But who should control them?

Virtually dead!

When someone dies, it is customary in many countries to announce the death publicly by placing a death notice or an obituary in newspapers. A number of "virtual graveyards" have sprung up on the Web that enable people to post virtual memorials or tributes to loved ones.

A sports photographer sends digital photographs from the field to his news agency by e-mail.

The list of uses the Internet has been put to is endless. Doctors in front-line military hospitals use it to e-mail test results, images of patients, and X rays to specialists for a second opinion. Family doctors and hospital specialists give consultations to patients using on-line video links. And governments use it to promote health care and give medical advice. Climbers take digital photographs on their way up the world's highest mountains and post them on web sites by satellite telephone. Internet news stories are updated round the clock, so news often breaks first on the Internet. So, when the first supersonic land speed record was set in the United States in 1997, digital photographs of the car and details of its speeds and times were available to the public on the team's web site within minutes.

DEBATE

Should anyone be able to put ideas, however wacky, on the World Wide Web for everyone to read? Or should crazy ideas be kept off the Web? In the past, some ideas that were thought to be completely crazy turned out to be true—for example, at one time it was considered madness to suggest that the earth was not flat and was not the center of the universe.

Trend spotting

The Net serves the needs of people, so it has to adapt to match changes in our society. As a result, ISPs are in a very good position to spot changing trends in society because of their direct, interactive (two-way) links with people through the Net. In the future, changes in the Net and the services that ISPs offer may be among the first clues to changes in society at large.

The way we see Net users is altering already. A survey of 2,000 school children in 1999 found that just over half of them (fifty-one percent) have used the Internet. More than half said they thought Internet users were smart. Nearly half (forty percent) thought Net users were fun. Only a twentieth (five percent) of the children thought that Net users were odd. The Net may once have been a refuge for young male computer nerds, but in less than ten years it has developed into something entirely different—a vast and diverse network that has attracted hundreds of millions of people by responding to their different needs.

Children growing up now are the first Internet generation.

FREEDOM OF INFORMATION

A Force for Democracy, or a Global Free-For-All?

Broadcasting and newspapers make it more difficult for repressive regimes to keep their people ignorant of national and international events. Even in countries where the press and media are tightly controlled, newspapers from free countries are smuggled in and radio broadcasts are picked up, bringing in news from the outside world. Telephones and fax machines enable information to travel more easily across borders from one person to another. The Internet takes this process of freeing information from political control further. It not only supports person-to-person communication by e-mail, it also enables a whole population to tap into international news and current affairs and to search for information on particular topics.

Visitors to a computer show in China line up to surf the Net. The number of people going on-line in China is growing fast.

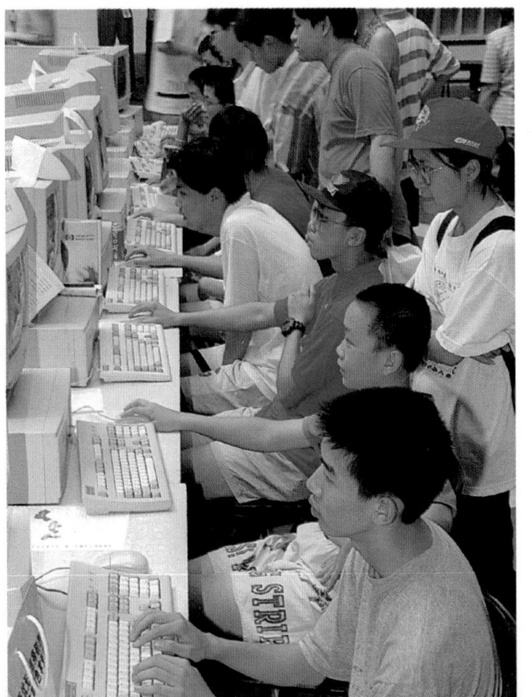

Some governments are so worried about the Internet and what their people might learn by using it that they are actively trying to stop people from accessing it. In North Korea, it is illegal for private citizens to use the Internet. In Burma, anyone who wants to use the Internet has to register with the police. In Malaysia, Internet cafés must keep a record of all customers using their Internet terminals. In other countries, including China, Vietnam, and Saudi Arabia, access to web sites that the government disapproves of for political, religious, or moral reasons, is blocked. But even if the government closes down a web site in one country, new versions of the site may be set up in other parts of the world. The Internet is very difficult for governments to censor.

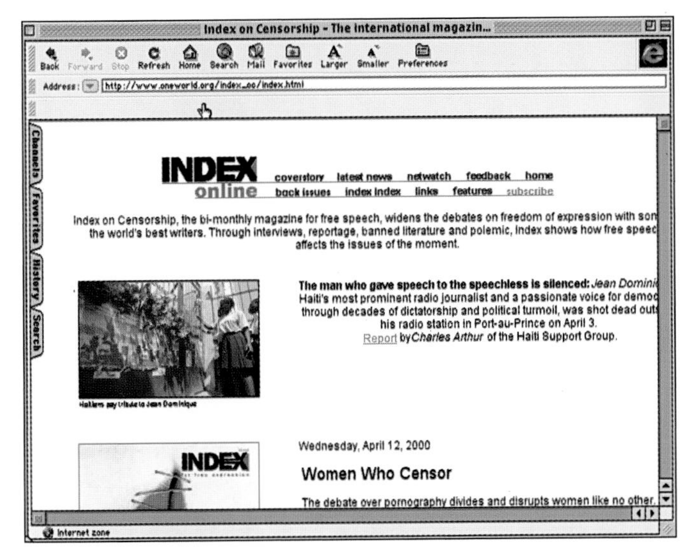

Should the Internet be censored or should there be freedom of expression? Index on Censorship provides an on-line magazine in favor of free speech. But there are many individuals, organizations, and governments that would like to control the Net.

In democratic societies people often disagree with some of the things their governments do. Minorities, who cannot achieve political change through the ballot box, may seek other ways to realize their ambitions. The Internet has become important to them too. Political activists seek to obtain coverage in the national press and broadcast news media to gain support for their aims. One way of ensuring coverage is to attract people to high-profile demonstrations. More people means greater coverage. To that end, there are web sites carrying news of forthcoming protests and demonstrations in the hope that like-minded people will see where and when the next event is to happen and attend it. Some groups who receive news coverage are unhappy about the way filmed reports are edited and broadcast, so they are fighting back by making their own video reports and releasing them on the Web, thus bypassing the broadcast media.

VIEWPOINTS

"The Net interprets censorship as damage and routes around it."
John Gilmore, writer and on-line freedom activist

"Most people believe that if you go in and try to micromanage a forest, it is possible to destroy the very things that make it a unique and special place. That's just as true of the Net."
Glen Raphael, computer software engineer and political theorist

The language barrier

If you speak English, cyberspace is a wonderful place. But what if you don't? English is the most widely used language on the Internet, because the Internet developed first and fastest in English-speaking countries. But it is predicted that Net users who are not native English speakers will dominate the Net by 2002. So English speakers surfing the Net are increasingly likely to come across web sites in non-English languages. Web sites often offer two or more language options. Usually one of them is English, so English-speaking surfers can access web sites originating from, say, Japan, or most Western European and Scandinavian countries.

It is becoming increasingly easy to get on-line. This businessman is surfing the Web in a Dutch hamburger spot that also offers phone and fax services to its customers.

There are computer programs that can translate one language into another. There are also web sites that make it possible to translate text among the world's major languages. In the future, on-line interpreters might be able to translate any web site from one language to another in real time—so that, say, for a Spanish speaker logging on to a German web site the site would appear translated automatically into Spanish.

Rare languages

Hundreds of rare, or lesser used, languages are spoken by a minority of people compared to the world's major languages. These languages include Catalan (spoken mainly in Spain and France), Sardinian (spoken on the island of Sardinia), Romansh (spoken in Switzerland), and Sami (spoken in northern Finland). The growth of the Internet, which encourages people to communicate in English, could drive these little-used languages out of existence. Alternatively, the Internet might have the opposite effect. It might actually save some of these endangered languages from extinction by enabling more of the people who speak them to communicate and keep them alive.

The cost of Internet access once prevented many people from going on-line. But now easier Internet access and, in some places, free access is bringing the Net within the reach of more people in both developed and developing nations. In Denmark, for example, the public can access the Internet free of charge at most public libraries. Anyone who can't afford to buy equipment can buy time on terminals at Internet bars and cafés. And access through television sets and mobile phones may also make the Internet available to people who don't want, or cannot afford, to buy a computer.

FACT

Half of the world's children are more than eight hours' walk from the nearest telephone.

The Internet could be used to distribute advice on health and hygiene in the developing world, if ways could be found for people to access it. This reluctant child is being weighed by a health worker.

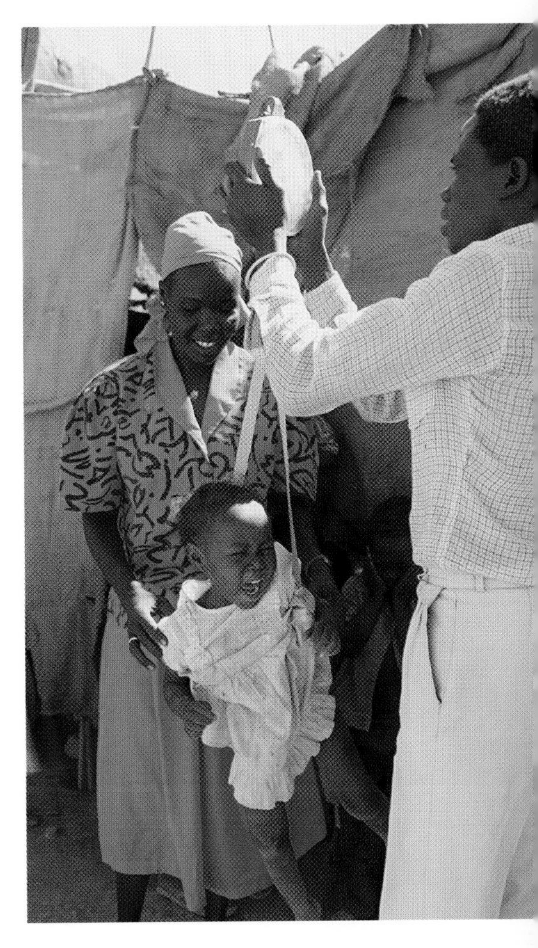

The situation is different in the developing world, where extreme poverty still prevents millions of people from joining the global on-line community. These people could benefit from basic information about health, hygiene, and medicine. Parents could be helped with child care advice. Farmers could receive help with agricultural problems. But villagers, parents, and farmers in developing countries rarely own computers or surf the Web.

A problem in Africa is that there are relatively few telephone lines, and many of the remote communities and sparsely inhabited places may never be cabled for communications. But there are hundreds of local radio stations across Africa and many of them have Internet access. They broadcast advice and information received via the Web to villagers who have radio sets. They can also relay answers to specific questions and appeals for help. In future, satellites may provide the communications services that are essential for widespread Internet connection across the African continent.

Bill Gates, who co-founded the giant Microsoft corporation in the 1970s. Microsoft's Windows operating system is used by most of the world's personal computers. Microsoft has also developed the Microsoft Network, a program for accessing the World Wide Web.

Fair competition?

More than ninety percent of the world's personal computers use Microsoft's Windows operating system. Microsoft's commercial rivals claim that this gives it an unfair advantage when it comes to supplying other software that works with Windows. They say that Microsoft's inside knowledge of forthcoming Windows developments gives it a head start in the production of Windows programs. Microsoft has also supplied its Internet browser, Internet Explorer, with Windows, which, its rivals say, is unfair because this makes it more difficult for them to sell their own browsers.

Competition between companies usually leads to better products and lower prices. Microsoft's rivals claim that its dominance of parts of the computer software market works against competition. The U.S. Department of Justice questioned Microsoft's business practices in the courts. Microsoft defended itself by claiming that its products are successful and widely used because they are superior products, and argued that it should not be penalized for this. The Department of Justice ruled that Microsoft should be split into two competing companies, a change that Microsoft has opposed and is contending.

Voting on-line

There is one human activity where millions of people all communicate information at roughly the same time—in elections. Most elections around the world involve polling stations where people mark their choice of candidate on paper slips, which are then deposited into locked boxes. All the slips are then transported to counting stations and counted by hand. In close-fought elections, candidates may ask for the votes to be counted again in case there have been any mistakes. It's a slow, labor-intensive process. Often, elections fail to attract voters in great numbers, and that is bad for democracy.

FACT

The world's first on-line election took place in March 2000 in Arizona. It was a primary within the Arizona Democratic Party.

Elections could be carried out electronically using the Internet from home or from Internet terminals in public places. If voting was as easy as sending an e-mail, more people might vote. There would need to be a foolproof way of identifying each voter to ensure that only people who are entitled to vote can register their vote, and that they vote only once. However, for an on-line voting system to be democratic, every citizen would need to have Internet access.

DEBATE

Can we trust on-line voting systems enough to use them to elect our governments, or is it safer to stick to low-technology voting systems?

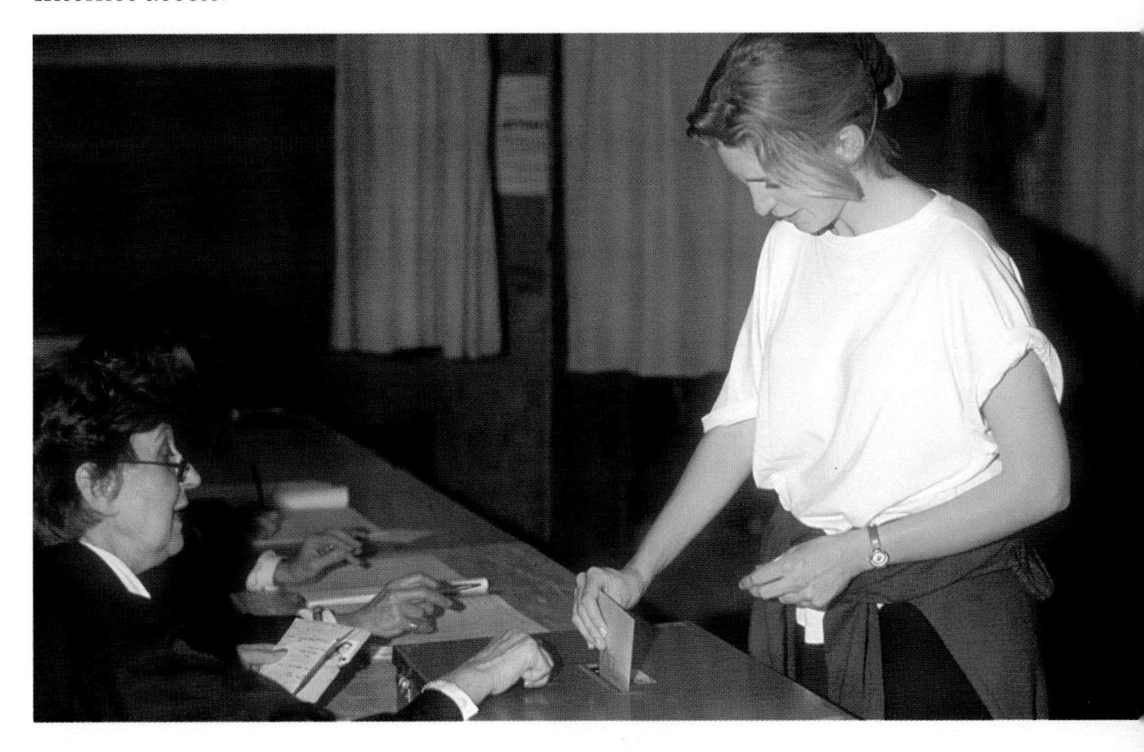

Today most people in the world vote by marking a cross next to a name on a piece of paper and putting it in a box. The Internet offers a way for people to vote electronically.

At the moment, accessing information on-line is a slow process. The World Wide Web is sometimes called the World Wide Wait by frustrated surfers waiting for pages to appear on their screens. But within a few years, Internet access speeds will rise dramatically as new high-speed digital connections by optical cable and, perhaps, by satellite become available. When that happens there will, in effect, be no limit to the amount of information that can be accessed.

GROWING UP WITH THE INTERNET

Dangerous Toy, or Educational Tool?

The Internet is a recent development, but it has burst upon the world's computer users so rapidly that it has gone from nowhere to everywhere within ten years. Younger children today have never known a world without the Internet. Children are growing up with the Internet as a perfectly normal part of their lives. In the future, the Internet may affect them in ways we can't imagine now.

Sony Station: multimedia corporation Sony's on-line entertainment center. After initially seeing the Internet as a threat, because of the ease with which music can be copied and downloaded digitally, the entertainment industry is now learning to work with it.

Chatting on-line

Chat rooms make it easy for people to get together on the Net. They work like e-mail, except that messages are seen by anyone who logs on to the same chat room. Any of the room's virtual visitors can answer messages, and their replies are seen on the screen instantly. Some people have found lasting friends, romance, and even marriage in on-line chat rooms. But dangerously, things can go wrong. You might think you're chatting with a fifteen-year-old who shares your interests and who might be nice to meet, but do you really know with whom you are communicating? A chat room lets people pretend to be whoever they want to be, for whatever reason. You might actually be chatting to a fifty-year-old man who would be distinctly dangerous to meet. So it's always a good idea not to reveal too much personal information when you're on-line.

News groups are another resource for exchanging news, information, and ideas with other people interested in the same things. There are about 25,000 news groups, collectively known as Usenet. Usenet is not part of the Internet, although most Internet Service Providers also provide access to Usenet. Each news group deals with a different topic. A news group has nothing to do with news—it is more like a bulletin board. All the messages sent to it are seen by anyone who logs on to that particular news group.

VIEWPOINT

"Don't think of people you chat to on-line as being people you know. They are still strangers. People can pretend and they do pretend."

Ann Davison, Director of ERICA (European Research Into Consumer Affairs)

Log on to fun

People have played games on the Internet since its earliest days. In the beginning, bored computer operators invariably played games on their machines. When the World Wide Web was invented, on-line games advanced quickly. Now you can log on to games producers' web sites and see demonstrations of new games. Or you can download games. And, as connections to the Internet have speeded up, it is now possible to play games on line. With even faster Internet connections, it should soon be possible to play games with more complex graphics and sound effects on-line.

Computer games of all sorts are now available from the Internet. You can try out new games on-line, download games on to your own computer, or even play games against other surfers.

If it becomes possible to play the most popular computer games on-line in real time without running up a monster phone bill, why bother going to the store to buy a game on disk? If on-line games-playing becomes the norm, it could have serious implications for stores that sell games. Perhaps stores that sell computer games will disappear altogether.

The learning zone

The Internet is an almost limitless source of information on every imaginable subject, so it is very useful for researching topics for school homework and projects. E-mail can come in handy too. When a British schoolgirl had to travel to Australia during the school year, she sent in her schoolwork by e-mail while she was away. In developed countries, the Internet-linked school is rapidly becoming the norm. A common problem connected with introducing the Internet to schools is that teachers may be less well acquainted with the Internet than the children they are teaching.

The Internet can be a useful tool in education, giving teachers and children access to new sources of information.

With the Internet, it is technically possible for a teacher to teach a class of children who never leave home. The children, at home, could be linked to the school via sound, video, and text Internet links. In Australia, children living in remote areas already take part in classes linked by radio. Using an Internet link could be the next step. But, for the rest of us, the Internet school is probably one development we will not see in our lifetimes. Most people agree that it is better for children to learn together, because socialization is an important part of growing up. The teaching of children alone at home, therefore, is not without its problems.

VIEWPOINT

"Imagine a school with children that can read or write, but with teachers who cannot, and you have a metaphor of the Information Age in which we live."
Peter Cochrane, journalist

The sheer volume of information on the Internet means that users need to exercise caution. It's important to remember that anyone can set up a web site and fill it with information. This information may be correct or it may be wrong. There is so much rubbish on the Internet that any researcher has to exercise caution and judgment when using it. Perhaps this is a good thing. In a future world awash with more news and information than ever before, all of us will have to learn to question more. If information is to be correct, it's important to ensure that it comes from a reliable source.

A reliable on-line source is much the same as any other good source. Information from a well-known encyclopedia or an official university site or news organization is likely to be reliable. Information from commercial companies may be biased toward that company's products. Information from a political party may be biased toward that party's policies. Information from individuals may be reliable or ridiculous.

A virtual gallery

The Internet is transforming museums and art galleries. Museums often have more objects in storerooms than on display. This may be simply because they don't have the floor space necessary, or it may be that some items are so fragile they need special storage conditions. Other items may be so valuable that the institution can't afford the security measures necessary to put them on public display. All of these items can be made available to everyone digitally. The British Library is currently digitizing many of its priceless books and documents so that they can be seen and studied by more people. In the same way, digital images of museum objects allow many more people to see them via computer. In 1999, about one million people visited the National Portrait Gallery in London. In the same period, a half million people looked at its web site.

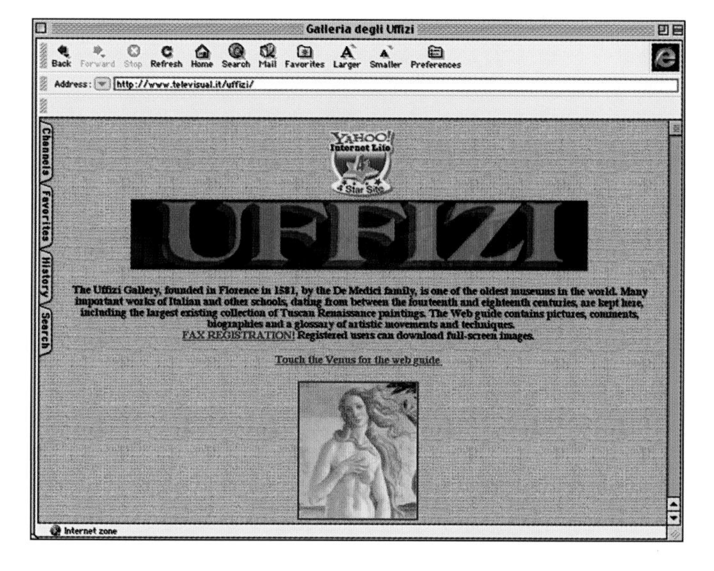

The Web enables people to access museums, art galleries, and libraries, such as the Uffizi gallery in Florence, Italy, or the University of Copenhagen Botanical Museum in Denmark—places that they may never have the opportunity to visit in person.

Lone surfers

Parents are often worried by the amount of time their children spend in front of a computer screen. The Internet has prompted similar concerns. Some people are worried that children who spend a lot of time communicating with others on-line are not making enough face-to-face contact with people. Some of the concerns arise from the belief that surfing is a lone activity, which conjures up the idea of thousands, perhaps millions, of children and teenagers alone in darkened rooms staring at computer screens. It's almost like a scene from a sinister science fiction movie. But is it what's actually happening?

VIEWPOINT

"...the more hours people use the Internet, the less time they spend with real human beings... "
Norman Nie, political scientist, Stanford University, California

Half of a group of children who took part in a 1999 survey said they surfed the Web with friends. About one fifth surfed with their fathers and a further tenth with their mothers. So, roughly eighty percent of the youngest group of the Internet generation sees surfing as a group activity, and they enjoy face-to-face interaction with other people even while they are surfing. That leaves about one out of five children surfing alone. Whether or not their lone surfing is a problem depends on factors such as the length of time they spend surfing alone, the type and suitability of the web sites they visit, and how much "normal" contact with other people they have when they're not surfing.

Museums and art galleries all over the world are making information about their collections and exhibits available on-line.

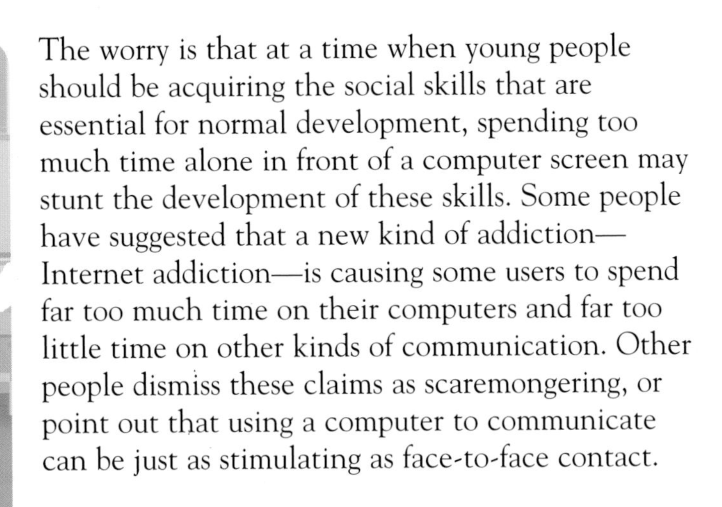

VIEWPOINTS

"The only valid censorship of ideas is the right of people not to listen."
Tommy Smothers, comedian

"Every imaginable type of filth and perversion is freely available [on the Internet]. It's our job to get rid of it."
Commissioner Karlheinz Moewes, Head of the Munich Internet police squad

The worry is that at a time when young people should be acquiring the social skills that are essential for normal development, spending too much time alone in front of a computer screen may stunt the development of these skills. Some people have suggested that a new kind of addiction—Internet addiction—is causing some users to spend far too much time on their computers and far too little time on other kinds of communication. Other people dismiss these claims as scaremongering, or point out that using a computer to communicate can be just as stimulating as face-to-face contact.

Filtering output

It is a commonly held belief, mainly among people who use the Web very little or not at all, that it is awash with violent and pornographic material from which children must be protected. There are indeed many web sites containing offensive material. There are web sites that show how to make weapons and there are sites that spread violent images, sexually explicit images, and racist propaganda. Between ten and twenty percent of children surveyed say that they have come across something on the Net that they found upsetting or embarrassing. The figures don't reveal the extent and nature of the upset and embarrassment, or whether the children came across the troubling material accidentally or deliberately searched for it, so it's hard to judge how serious the problem is. However, the proportion is worryingly high.

Parents and educators naturally want to screen out

Some of the views expressed on the Web are extreme and offensive to many people. Should the views of racists, such as these members of the Ku Klux Klan, be aired via the Internet? Or should they be censored?

offensive material. A variety of computer programs, nicknamed censorware or blocking software, has been developed to filter out offensive material automatically. But some of this blocking software can cause problems. A blocking program that simply scans web sites for offensive words works well most of the time, but it may also stop a computer from logging on to web sites that include references to innocent topics such as *breast* stroke swimming, *breast* cancer, *naked* eye astronomy, paint *stripping* and so on. Place names can also sometimes have unfortunate groups of letters within them that cause them to be blocked. When examples like this are discovered, the sites can be unblocked. The types of web sites that are blocked are sometimes controversial. Blocking programs have sometimes been used to block web sites associated with feminist or gay rights issues, topics that many people feel should not be blocked.

DEBATE

Should decisions about Net content deemed to be unsuitable for children be taken by parents or by governments? Should there simply be a minimum age for access to the Internet that keeps children off-line?

Web sites that deal with different lifestyles, politics, and interests often serve as a focus for like-minded people to express their views. People who oppose or disapprove of them sometimes block these sites from their computer systems.

E-BUSINESS

Breaking Economic Barriers, or Winner Takes All?

E-commerce is growing fast. All sorts of products and services for individuals and businesses are now available on the Web.

In the volatile, fast-changing markets of the twenty-first century, the company with the quickest response time is the one most likely to succeed. The Internet enables businesses to respond to customers' needs and changing circumstances faster than ever.

Many businesses have their own web sites, and some of them have an e-mail facility so that people can contact the company on-line. At first, businesses used web sites to advertise their products and services—many still do. Customers can access information twenty-four hours a day, seven days a week. Then, when it became possible to buy things over the Net, businesses slowly started doing business electronically. This is called e-business, or e-commerce. It enables customers to download product information and place orders twenty-four hours a day. E-commerce is now growing rapidly.

Done in an instant

Design companies have found the Net particularly useful. Everything around us is designed—and the designs usually have to be agreed upon by several people in a number of different places. E-mail allows designs to be sent anywhere in the world for approval: a manufacturer based in a town in Denmark, for example, can send designs across the Internet to a manufacturing plant in Korea just as easily as to the nearest town.

Large construction projects may require thousands of design drawings. The drawings are never perfect first time. They frequently need to be changed, and all the changes have to be approved before they are passed on to the construction engineers. The communications speed provided by the Internet makes this possible without bringing the project to a halt. It also means that designers are no longer called upon to redraw scores of drawings manually after every change. All the drawings are linked electronically; by updating one drawing, a designer automatically updates all the others that are affected, making huge savings in time and expense.

VIEWPOINT

"Most of us are fast getting used to the convenience of 24-hour shopping. As our lives get busier, it will soon cease to be a bonus and seem more like a necessity."
Andrew Nowell, UUNET (an Internet service provider)

Small is beautiful

A person looking at a company's web site can't always tell whether the company in question is a tiny one-person outfit, a national chain, or a multinational. So the Web helps small companies to compete with large companies on more equal terms. It also enables small companies to contact customers all over the world directly, very easily and inexpensively. This means that companies that sell to the public no longer need a prime main street location from which to trade.

Designs for everything, from paperclips to skyscrapers, are sent out to clients, contractors, and manufacturers by e-mail in a fraction of the time it takes to send drawings on paper by mail or courier.

In some ways, the Net is exercising an equalizing influence on society. Many of the injustices in society are caused when groups of people are excluded or discriminated against or denied power, information, or wealth. The Net can help to remove barriers such as race, age, social class, or sex. In cyberspace, you can't see the color of someone's skin or discern his or her age, religion, or social class. You can't always be certain whether the person you're communicating with is male or female.

Surfers try out the Net at the 1998 World Internet conference in New Delhi, India.

In some countries, the Middle East for example, strictly observed social conventions, religious beliefs, or laws exclude women from participating in many activities as freely and easily as men. The Internet enables women in these countries to access and use information and services on an equal basis with men, without venturing beyond the existing conventions of those countries. However, given the relative ease of access to the Internet in the developed world, there may be danger that developing countries will be left behind in the race toward a global Internet-based economy.

VIEWPOINT

"Those economies with access to modern communication networks will clearly develop much faster than those without. The Internet will increase the divide between developed and developing countries."
David Powell, a consultant with an Internet investment bank

On the Net, people can compete with one another on merit, regardless of who or what they are or where they come from. Entrepreneurs in Asia, the Middle East, and Latin America have realized this and they are using the Internet to get into businesses and markets that, until recently, were dominated by North American and European companies. They can do this because the Net enables businesses to be based anywhere. It no longer matters what a company's address is—what matters is the quality of its work. It was once necessary for a company to be based near a community of similar businesses: for example, Silicon Valley in California. But now that company can just as easily be based in a small town in India. Indian programmers and web site designers are in great demand because the quality of their work is equal to the best in the world, but labor costs and overhead, the other costs associated with running businesses, are much lower.

VIEWPOINTS

"The Net can't act as the great equalizer unless everyone has equal access to it."
From "Mapping a Virtual Planet," **Newsweek**, *by Rana Dogar and Carla Power*

"New computing and communications technologies offer an unprecedented chance to create vast new markets while lifting billions out of poverty."
Iqbal Z. Quadir in **Newsweek**

Virtual businesses

The Internet enables small companies with different skills in design, project management, materials science, computing, communications, manufacturing, and so on to work closely together—so closely, in fact, that they form a "virtual business." This is a business that exists only because of the Internet links holding it together. Companies can reach out to each other across the Internet like the many-branched connections of brain cells, developing new relationships and exchanging information, breaking some connections and making new ones in a more complex and flexible way than was possible before.

Wherever you happen to be in the world, your office can link up with others through the Internet and form a virtual business.

Following the Sun

International businesses with offices all around the world have discovered a way of using the Internet to increase their problem-solving power. Problems occur daily, especially in high technology companies. A problem that arises at one office is worked on at that office. If it isn't solved by the end of that day, it's posted on the company's intranet (a network that works in the same way as the Internet, but can be accessed only by the company that created it, not by the public).

The Internet gives businesses the opportunity to work around the clock. These Japanese office workers can send projects to their colleagues in Europe who, because of the time difference, will work on them while Japan sleeps.

As the earth turns and the sun goes down, one office shuts and another one elsewhere opens for business. The staff looks at any problems posted on the company's intranet, and add their thoughts. The sun sets, and that office closes. Yet another opens, and so on. By the time the office that originally posted the problem opens again the next day, the problem has been worked on around the clock and probably solved by people in several different countries.

Taking risks

The Internet enables people to do things for themselves that used to be done with the help of professionals and experts. Booking vacations on-line, instead of using an expert adviser such as a travel agent, involves few extra risks. There are some on-line services, however, that are much more risky—trading on the stock market.

One way of investing money, in order to make more money, is to buy shares in a company. Share buyers are entitled to share in a company's profits (and losses). If the value of the company rises on the stock market, share owners can sell their shares for a higher price than they paid and make a profit. The value of a company rises or falls from minute to minute throughout the day. It is set according to the number of people wanting to invest in the company and how much money they are prepared to pay. If lots of people want to buy shares, the company's value rises. If people start selling their shares, its value falls.

On-line dealing in stocks is becoming increasingly popular, but it is a very risky hobby for inexperienced people.

Shares used to be bought and sold by agreement between professional dealers, called brokers, who contacted each other in person or by telephone. It took time to make deals. But share buying and selling has gone electronic and on-line. It's now easier than ever for ordinary people to buy and sell shares. However, share dealing is a form of gambling and if the gambles don't pay off, there can be substantial losses. So just because a service is available on the Net doesn't mean that it is advisable for surfers to use it.

Millions of shares are also bought and sold using computers programmed to react more quickly to changes in share values than human dealers can. These computers protect the companies who have bought the shares, and prevent them from losing money by buying or selling shares before anyone else can react to changing prices. The computers can trigger an avalanche of instant share selling, which may make share values drop like a stone. The Internet's ability to connect these computers worldwide can amplify the effect and turn a fall in prices into a stock market crash.

DEBATE

Will e-commerce push small, local companies out of business as their clients look farther afield for more profitable trading partners? Or will it enable such companies to prosper by attracting a wealth of new clients?

NET CRIME

An Aid for Detectives, or Criminal Heaven?

VIEWPOINT

"The Information Age has brought us different threats to the safety of women and children."
Al Gore, U.S. Vice President

Criminals play a never-ending game of cat-and-mouse with police forces. New advances in technology are soon taken up by criminals to gain an advantage over the police and other criminals. The Internet is no exception. It enables criminals to reach more people more quickly than was ever possible before. Cyber-crime, as it is called, is also attractive to criminals because it can be committed a long way away from the victim. Cyber-criminals don't need guns, masks, or getaway cars. They do, however, need to have advanced technological skills. And they may inadvertently leave traces of their activities which allow the police to track them down. If caught, they may face penalties as serious as those for "real-life" crimes.

Hacking

Hacking is probably the best-known cyber-crime. It involves getting around the security measures that protect commercial, scientific, government, and military computer systems. Once inside a system, hackers look at secret files and sometimes alter the information they contain. The Internet gives hackers access to thousands of computers worldwide.

Some computer systems are very poorly protected against hacking because, in certain cases, their owners or operators don't think anyone could possibly be interested in their contents. An American university discovered that it needed greater computer security when a student hacked into one of its computers and changed the exam results of fellow students he didn't like from passes to failures!

More than half of the companies who took part in a recent survey in the United States said that they had been attacked by hackers using Internet connections—a rise from one third in 1996. Computer systems are often protected by passwords. Hackers know that people tend to choose passwords that are easy to remember. These may be obvious words that are easy for a hacker to guess. One survey found that half of people who were questioned chose their partner's name as their password. The hardest passwords to guess are words that have nothing to do with the system or the information they protect, or consist of random sequences of letters, numbers and punctuation.

A scene from the 1995 movie, Hackers, *about a group of young people who break into protected computer systems. The Internet gives hackers access to thousands of computers all over the world.*

Hackers also know that the computer programmers who produce programs for protected systems often write something called a "back door" into the program. Back doors give programmers a quick way into a program without going through all the front end security built into the system. If a program is disabled by a computer crash, the programmer can still get in through the back door and work on it. The hacker looks for back doors, like a thief looking for a house key hidden under a plant-pot outside a house.

Ehud Tenenbaum, also known as "the Analyzer," was identified by the Federal Bureau of Investigation (FBI) as the hacker who accessed the Pentagon's computer system in Washington DC in 1998.

Hackers also know that some organizations have very tight computer security, but fail to look after "traditional" security. An employee may sometimes write down a password on a scrap of paper and leave it in a desk drawer—just for convenience. A criminal who gets into an office, perhaps posing as a cleaner or worker, may be able to find these password notes and use them later to access the system remotely via the Internet.

Companies and web sites can be attacked and forced off-line without having their security measures breached. In February 2000, a number of well-known on-line companies, including the search engine Yahoo and the bookseller Amazon, were forced off-line for several hours at a time by the sheer number of "hits" (visits from surfers) they were receiving. Every web site is operated by computer systems called servers and communications switches called routers, which can only make a certain number of telephone connections at a time. Malicious surfers appeared to be using computer programs to bombard these web sites with so many hits that their systems could not cope.

This is a very worrying development, because it means that any web site can be attacked at any time. At first thought it appears to be the cyber equivalent of what has always happened in the real world. Any store, office, company, laboratory, or military establishment may find itself targeted by protesters who can bring work to a halt. But there is a big difference between the two. People who protest and demonstrate in person usually want to air a grievance in order to exercise more leverage on an organization. On the other hand, cyber attacks are more like aimless vandalism. They seem to come from nowhere from people who may just be doing it out of malice. Such attacks are much more difficult to combat.

FACT

In 1994, a hacker was dubbed "the number one threat to United States' security" by the Central Intelligence Agency. The hacker had breached the security of top-secret U.S. military intelligence systems no less than two hundred times. The crimes were eventually traced to a sixteen-year-old schoolboy in London!

Copyright

Almost everything that is written, drawn, sung, performed, or photographed is owned by someone. Or, rather, the right to publish it or sell it is owned by someone. For example, a newspaper is allowed to publish a photograph or part of a book only if it has the permission of the copyright owner, who might well ask for payment. Using someone's work without permission is called copyright infringement, and is against the law. Clip art sold to computer users is one exception. This can be used without payment. Now that it is possible to distribute text, pictures, and music around the world digitally, it can be very difficult to keep track of who is using them and where, and if they are entitled to do so. Pop music in particular is at risk of illegal copying across the Internet.

President Bill Clinton meets with heads of the computer technology industry to propose a new Internet security plan following a hacker attack on leading web sites in February 2000.

The biggest copyright infringement problem is undoubtedly software piracy. Computer programs and the packaging they are sold in are very easy to copy. The U.S. Software Publishers Association estimates that about $7.4 billion worth of software was lost to piracy in 1998. The Association also found more than 1,500 examples of illegal software being offered for sale on the Internet.

In 1999, Europe's biggest software piracy operation was traced to Denmark and shut down. It had produced 125,000 counterfeit CD-ROMs containing $237 million worth of various well-known computer programs. The pirated programs were advertised for sale on the Internet. Investigators received a tip that illegal CD-ROMs were being sold through a Danish web site. The Danish police acted swiftly to close down the Internet outlets and arrest the criminals. Leading software producers take the problem of piracy so seriously that they have set up an international investigation team to track down software pirates.

Fraud

Fraud is a crime that involves cheating people out of money or goods. Fraud can take many forms, but some cases involve the illegal use of credit cards on the Internet. Buying something on the Internet by giving a credit card number is very straightforward. Unfortunately, criminals can get hold of genuine credit card numbers very easily. They might steal numbers from shopping receipts or credit card bills, or they might use a card number generator site on the Web. (Card number generators can automatically produce a valid-looking credit card number.) The card numbers are then used to buy things and the cost is charged to the cards' real owners. Credit card companies are trying to improve security to stop this. They are working toward real-time, on-line card authorization,

FACT

The North American Securities Administrators' Association estimates that U.S. investors lose $10 billion per year to Internet fraud—that's $1 million an hour!

sending goods only to the card account address; this would weed out fraud involving false card numbers, stolen card numbers, and stolen cards.

Another financial scam made easier by the Internet involves manipulating the value of a company's shares. Rumors that a company is doing particularly well or badly, or that it is about to take over another company or be taken over itself, can send share values up or down. One type of share fraud involves buying shares in a company, starting rumors that raise share values, and then selling the shares to make a profit.

Now anyone can buy and sell shares on the Internet. And e-mail can place rumors on selected people's computer screens. Sounds unlikely? In 1999, an American computer engineer was arrested for the first known example of this crime.

FACT

Only two percent of total credit card business involves Internet transactions, but these transactions result in fifty percent of all disputed credit card bills.

Goods are bought very easily on the Web by selecting products from a web site and paying for them by keying in a credit card number.

The Colombo stock exchange in Sri Lanka opens for business after a bomb attack by terrorists in 1999. Organizations like this, which depend heavily on computers and the Internet, are increasingly likely to be attacked electronically instead of with guns or bombs.

When he faked an Internet news story of a rumored billion dollar take-over of a company, its share value rose by thirty-one percent. He owned shares in the company and allegedly planned to sell them to make a profit. He was identified by FBI agents, who tracked his activities on the Internet.

The international nature of the Internet makes fraud easy to commit. In Europe a popular scam involves taking deposits for high-value goods, such as cars: the cars are sourced in one country, where car prices are low, and supplied to customers in another country where the same models sell for much higher prices. There are legitimate companies that specialize in this service, but it is also an area in which criminals operate. Buyers attracted by advertisements on web sites operated by fake import companies are kept waiting for weeks, sometimes months, while the criminals continue to collect deposits. Then the criminals simply disappear.

FACT

Complaints to the United States' Federal Bureau of Investigation (FBI) about Internet fraud are doubling every year—4,000 in 1997, 8,000 in 1998, 8,000 in the first half of 1999.

Sex on the Net

There is a lot of sexually explicit material on the Internet. But, in the same way that offensive books, magazines, and videos don't leap into your hands as soon as you walk into a store, sexually explicit images on the Net don't usually appear on a computer screen unless someone goes looking for them. The international nature of the Internet and the freedom of information flowing across national borders create problems for police forces dealing with crimes associated with sexually explicit material. As the Net is international, and laws governing sexually explicit material vary greatly from country to country, it is possible to view and download images that are legal in the place in which they are created and stored, but illegal in the place where they are accessed. Parents who are concerned that their children might access this material, whether deliberately or not, can use safeguards provided either by their Internet Service Provider or by a separate program to block it.

FACT

One of the most bizarre Internet crimes involved a man who offered money on the Web to have certain people killed. In 1999, police in England were alerted to a web site that contained a message offering payment to anyone who would "terminate" a named American couple. The message was traced and the man who placed it was arrested.

Some people have suggested that Internet Service Providers should be held legally responsible for the material communicated across their networks, or that they should censor it before it is made available to the public. This is rather like saying that the post office should be prosecuted for delivering letters that contain offensive material and that they should check every letter and take out anything that is pornographic. ISPs say that it is practically impossible to vet every web site, every scrap of downloaded material and every e-mail on their systems.

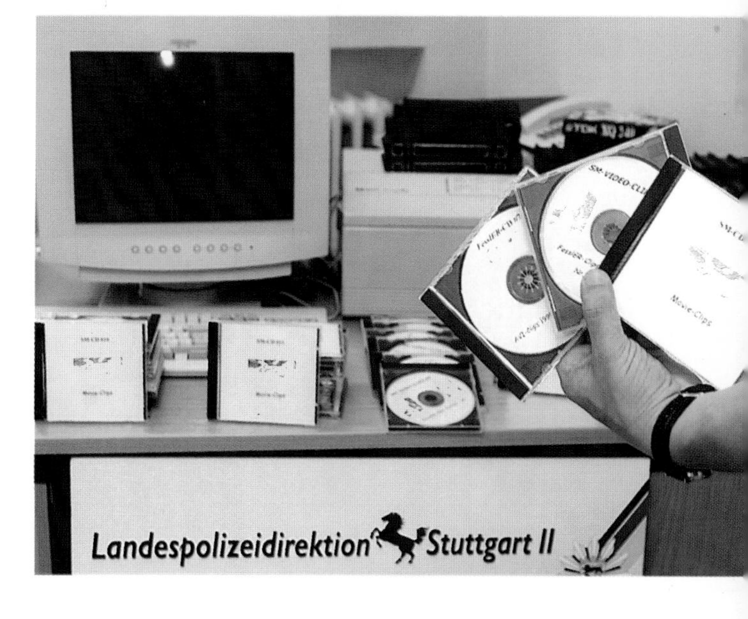

Computer disks containing indecent pictures of children are seized in Germany in 1998, after an investigation that resulted in 100 arrests of Internet-linked criminals in twelve countries.

Checking all this data in real time as it whizzes across the Net would slow down the whole network at a time when the ISPs are under great pressure to speed up access. And to make all the material acceptable everywhere, the standard of acceptability would presumably have to be set according to the most restrictive laws in any territory where the material could end up. It would destroy freedom of expression on the Net.

Virus busting

One of the most damaging computer crimes involves planting harmful programs called viruses in computer systems. Once a computer is infected, the virus might simply display a picture or message on the screen, or it might corrupt or erase files. It might not start working immediately. It might wait for a particular date to arrive or for a particular program to be started.

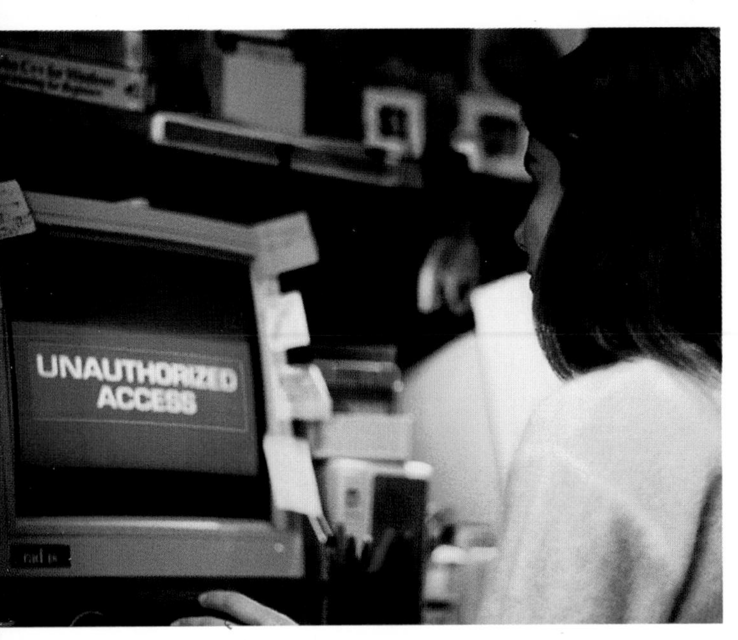

In the 1995 movie The Net, *a computer analyst battles with a program that gathers secret data and spreads false information.*

Before the Internet became so popular, viruses were often spread by infected disks that were unwittingly passed around between computer users. The first computer networks provided a new and more direct way for viruses to spread from one computer to another. And now the Internet provides a way for viruses to spread around the whole planet. Hundreds of new viruses are launched every month. There are also virus scares and hoaxes, which can be as damaging and time-consuming to deal with as the real thing. Specialist anti-virus companies continually search for new viruses and write anti-virus software to eliminate them.

FACT

According to the Taiwanese Defense Ministry's Information and Communications Bureau, Taiwan is reported to have about 1,000 computer viruses that it could use to defend itself against an attack from mainland China.

Viruses are often spread on the Internet as e-mail attachments—files that have to be opened to see what they contain. Opening the attachment triggers the virus. One of the most devastating computer viruses in recent years was called Melissa. Launched on the Internet in 1999, it was devastating because it didn't wait for a computer user to pass it on. It spread itself by e-mail—and fast. When a computer received the virus, the virus automatically mailed itself to the first fifty addresses stored in the computer's e-mail address book. And when it reached each of those fifty computers, it mailed itself to another fifty, and so on.

By clogging up e-mail systems with thousands upon thousands of e-mails, so that companies had to close down their systems, Melissa is estimated to have caused about $80 million of damage. An even more devastating virus was unleashed from the Philippines in 2000. Called the Lovebug (it was spread by an e-mail message titled "I love you") it e-mailed itself to everyone in the computer's address book. It spread around the world within hours, causing computer systems from the U.S. Department of Defense to the British House of Commons to shut down.

Writing a computer virus is a high-risk activity that may result in a lengthy prison sentence. Viruses are so effective at disabling computer systems that some governments are investigating their use as weapons to disable their enemies' computers.

David Smith is released on bail from Newark Federal Court in New Jersey after pleading guilty to spreading the Melissa virus in 1999.

VIEWPOINT

"The myth of the Internet is that people think it is an anonymous medium, that they cannot be traced."

Ruth Dixon, acting Chief Executive of the Internet Watch Foundation

Cyber-stalking

Continually following someone, sending him or her letters, or unwanted presents, or making unwelcome phone calls is called stalking. If the Internet is used, the crime is known as cyber-stalking.

In 1999, the first man in the United States to be found guilty of cyber-stalking was sentenced to six years in prison. A woman had rejected his advances, so he placed notices pretending to be a female in on-line chat rooms. When men answered his notices by e-mail, he invited them to the real woman's home. She often had to call the police for protection when the men arrived. Her father made the first breakthrough in the case by finding the stalker's notices and answering them himself. Once he had received e-mails from the cyber-stalker, the local police called in the FBI, who were able to trace the man who had sent them.

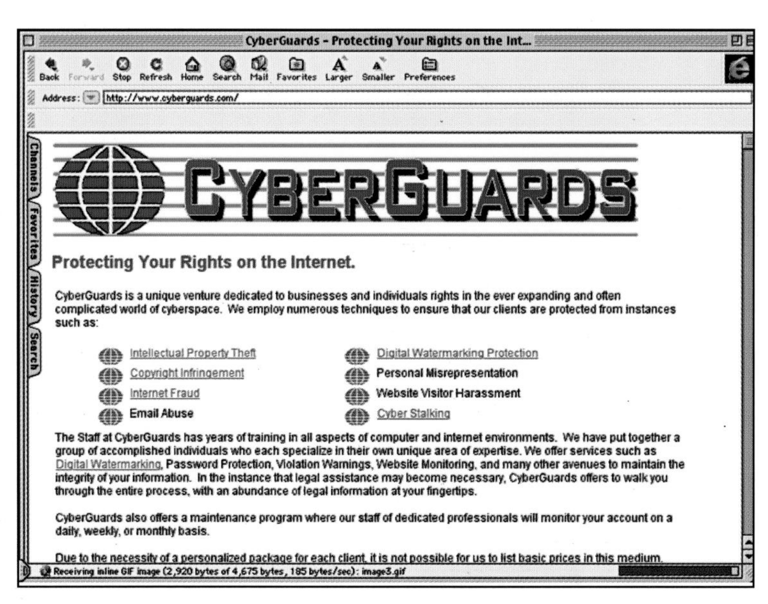

Cyber-stalking has become such a problem, especially in the United States, that there are web sites offering advice to people who think they may be the victims of cyber-stalkers.

Another cyber-stalker sent threatening e-mail to university students and their families. The police caught him by tracking his e-mails. All the e-mail was sent from one particular computer room. The police placed hidden cameras in the room and waited for the next e-mail to be sent. When the man came to send another e-mail, his image was recorded on video and then it was a simple matter of identifying him and picking him up.

Cyber-terrorism

Governments of technically advanced nations continually watch for the first signs of an attack by cyber-terrorists. These terrorists use the Internet in several ways. They use it as a source of information —on weapons suppliers and bomb-making, for example. They use it as a communications channel to exchange messages. And they use it as a weapon itself, to attack organizations.

Governments and military forces use secure communications channels and Internet sites, which should be able to resist penetration by terrorists. But, especially in the United States, there are thousands of government and military web sites that the general public can access. These public access points could let in the cyber-terrorists.

Fears of attacks by cyber-terrorists prompted the Pentagon to close down many public web sites at U.S. military establishments at the end of 1999. Each military establishment may have up to thirty

The Federal building in Oklahoma City, lies in ruins after a bomb attack in 1995. Governments are concerned about the availability of information on bombs and other weapons on the Web that might be used by terrorists.

VIEWPOINT

"There are some very smart people out there who are miles ahead of the law enforcement authorities, but thankfully criminals still use landlines."
Mark Steels, National Criminal Intelligence Service, UK

or forty public web sites. Most of them offer e-mail access, and this is where cyber-terrorists could gain a toehold in the system, perhaps to plant a damaging virus. The U.S. government felt that military web sites could be particularly vulnerable over the millennium weekend because of weaknesses that might be caused by the millennium bug. At the same time, secure military sites, including those operated by the Pentagon itself, kept going. In the event, the millennium bug seems to have had very little effect and there were no reports of cyber attacks.

Cyber-cops

Cyber-crime is a tricky problem for the police. Most police forces operate within state, county, regional, or national boundaries, while cyber-crime is often international. And it involves the sort of computer and communications technology that few police officers are expert in using. But cyber-crime is such an important and growing problem that police forces all over the world are now beginning to set up dedicated cyber-crime task forces to combat it.

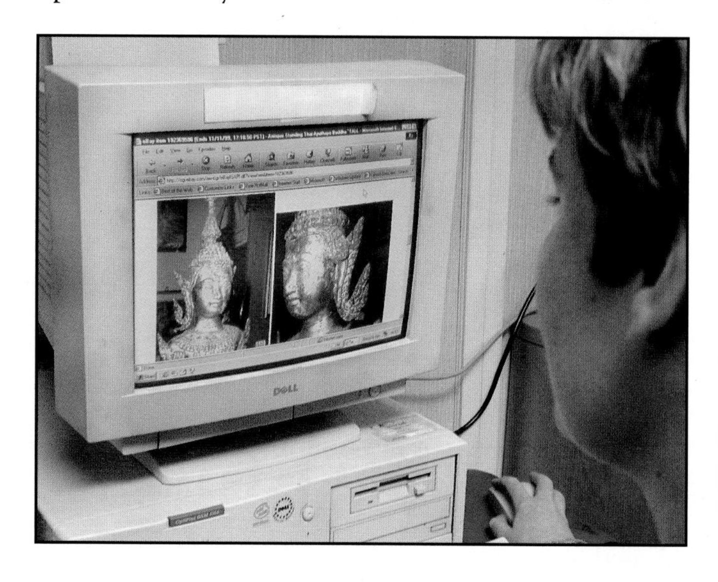

Cyber-crime is a big problem for businesses worldwide. Here in Bangkok, a woman looks at Thai antiques on an Internet auction site. Art theft and illegal sale of antiquities have increased substantially with easy access to the Internet.

Police forces in different countries have always collaborated to solve high-profile international crimes and particular types of crime, such as complex financial crimes, but Internet crime requires more international cooperation than ever between specialist Internet crime teams. In 1995, a police investigation into pedophile activities, called Operation Starburst, resulted in arrests leading to more than one hundred prosecutions in the United States, Great Britain, the Far East, and South Africa. Businesses take cyber-crime so seriously that the International Chamber of Commerce, the world's leading group of private businesses in 130 countries, has set up a specialist international anti-cyber-crime unit to provide a source of intelligence for police forces worldwide.

FACT

In Great Britain, figures released by the National Criminal Intelligence Service (NCIS) indicate that complaints to the police involving all types of cyber-crime rose from 12,000 in 1997 to more than 40,000 in 1998.

Police forces are learning how to use the Internet to track down criminals.

Crime on the Net is obviously a serious problem, raised to a great extent by the vast potential of the technology and the virtually unlimited amount of information on offer. While freedom of speech and the protection of privacy are important human rights that need to be safeguarded, we must ask if there are any instances where access to information should be limited. A world in which cyber-terrorists and pedophiles roam the Net unchecked is a frightening vision indeed.

DEBATE

Should all Internet communications be tagged electronically to identify the sender, so that law enforcement agencies can trace criminals more quickly and easily? Or should we defend our right to communicate electronically without being tracked by the authorities?

FUTURE DEVELOPMENTS

Full of Hope, or Full of Fear?

We look to the future as explorers standing on the shore of an uncharted ocean. Science, technology, politics, fashion, and world events all affect the course it will take. For that reason, crystal ball gazers often get it wrong. But perhaps there are a few things we can be reasonably sure about.

The growth of e-commerce is changing traditional main street stores and businesses. Internet business worldwide is valued at about $1 trillion, and it is growing fast. Some of that will be new business, because it's just so easy to buy and sell on-line. But a lot of it will be at the expense of traditional

In-store shopping may change forever because of the growth of e-commerce.

downtown stores. The businesses that will be affected most will probably be suppliers of video, music, and text—the easiest products to deliver digitally.

The trip to the store to rent a video could be a thing of the past within ten years. Cable and satellite television companies already offer pay-per-view blockbuster movies to their customers, but viewers have to wait until the next time the movie is transmitted. Now, one company has developed a digital video archive. There is no need to move from your armchair if you want to rent a film. Just select the movie from a menu on the TV screen and it is delivered digitally when you want it.

The music business is likely to be transformed more than most. The Internet enables record companies to sell music direct to customers without any need to make CDs and ship them to record stores. At least one major recording company is already considering doing this. But the record companies themselves could be in trouble. Big stars in the music business no longer need a record company to promote their music to the public. The singers and groups can sell music direct to people worldwide through their own web sites. Some new groups who are unable to get a recording contract are already doing this.

Oddly, book publishing, which you think would suffer most from the advent of the digital market place, has probably benefited more from it than any other medium to date. One of the first large product-selling businesses on the Web was Amazon, a company that sells books on-line. It is possible to dispense with publishers and printers altogether and publish on the Web instead. *Riding the Bullet*, a story by best-selling writer Stephen King, was published exclusively on the Web in March 2000. But demand exceeded the

VIEWPOINTS

"Looking at the proliferation of personal Web pages on the Net, it looks as if very soon everyone on earth will have fifteen megabytes of fame."
M. G. Siriam

"I'm curious to see what sort of response there is [to books published on-line] and whether or not this is the future."
Stephen King, writer

FACT

The Korean electronics company, Samsung, is developing a microwave oven that can connect to the Internet. It logs onto the food company web sites, reads the cooking instructions it finds there, and then cooks the food according to the instructions.

capacity of the web sites to deliver. When two million people tried to access the story, the web sites crashed.

In the near future, however, on-line publishing is unlikely to replace books. Even in this digital age, a book is still an efficient way to store large amounts of information in an easily accessible form. And the pleasure of holding a real book and leafing through its pages is not matched by gazing at words on a computer screen. But later generations may think differently. Perhaps they will be glad to be rid of dusty, bulky books in favor of text on disks or delivered on-line. Perhaps the future of book publishing is already here. At the beginning of 2000, software giant Microsoft and bookseller Barnes and Noble announced plans to develop electronic books that can be read on a palm-sized computer. The computer will be able to store several books at a time. In the future, books might be downloaded from the Internet.

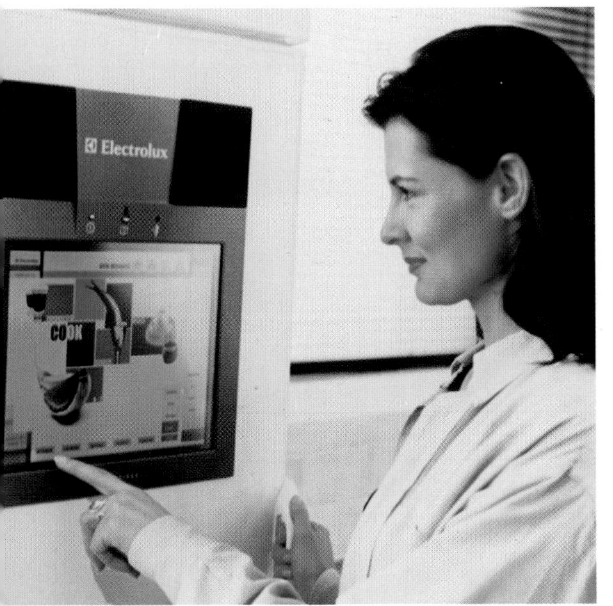

In the future, household appliances, like this refrigerator, will be linked to the Internet.

Machines on-line

The biggest growth in Internet traffic will not come from people, but from machines going on-line! About 500 million devices are on-line now, including 100,000 cameras. That figure is set to explode as more and more ordinary everyday devices are manufactured with built-in Internet links. Some will be connected to the telephone line while others will use mobile telephone technology to get on-line by radio. For years, people have been predicting washing machines that can send reports of their own faults to the manufacturer and central-heating systems that are remote-controlled, but Internet-linked machines might just be about to make all this finally

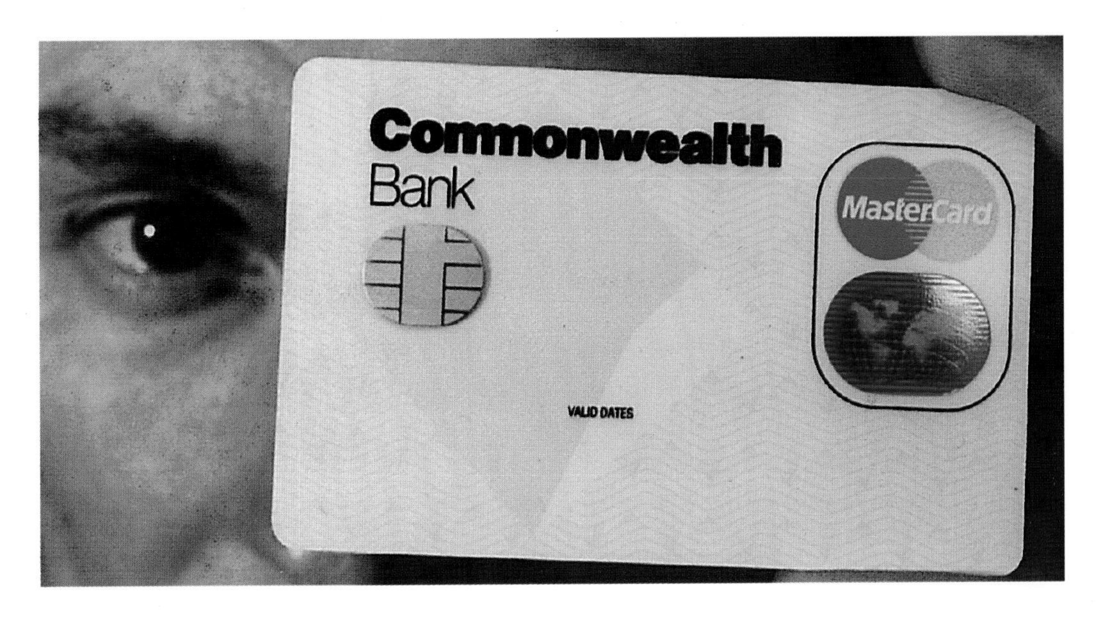

It is now possible to transmit "virtual money" across the Internet. Soon, this data will exist solely on a smart card, such as this British bank card.

come true. And, as the number of machines on-line grows and exceeds the number of people on-line, Web companies that now compete for human surfers' attention will begin to target machines.

Money, money, money

Until now, money on the move has always had to travel through banks or other established financial institutions. The Internet changes that. In the future, money could flow from smart card to smart card across the Internet without going through a bank. Freeing money from the banking system would certainly let money travel faster and more easily, but the Internet is unregulated, uncontrolled. It has none of the safeguards that are built into the international banking system to protect money from misuse. Money moving across the Internet electronically, out of the control of banks and other financial institutions, is more liable to fall prey to the attention of Internet fraudsters. And of course, direct cash transfers across the Internet make it more difficult for governments to tax the money and impossible for banks to make charges for handling it.

FACT

There is already a prototype of a refrigerator that is linked to the Internet. As each product in it is taken out and used, the refrigerator reads its barcode and when more of anything is needed, the refrigerator automatically adds it to a shopping order, which is sent to an on-line supermarket by e-mail.

VIEWPOINTS

"I worry that in ten to fifteen years from now, my child will come to me and say 'Daddy, where were you when they took freedom of the press away from the Internet?'"
Mike Godwin, lawyer, writer, and former counsel for the Electronic Frontier Foundation

"The Internet is the first limitless medium, and by its very nature, no single company or group can hope to control it."
Scott Miller, Communications Director, Time Warner

Electronic tracking

Every advance in technology has two sides. Combining the power of computers and the lightning speed of communications has brought undoubted benefits, but there is a dark side to the Net too. When you visit a web site you leave a digital calling card that identifies you. And then every time you visit the same web site, the site knows that it's you. A site that sells products, books for example, can build up a profile of your interests and recommend new books you might like to buy when you next log onto the site. The dark side of this technology is the ability secretly to compile other types of information about people by tracing the web sites they visit. Businesses could use the power of the Web to access, combine and analyze information about people in order to sell more products. Furthermore, political parties, governments, police forces, or even blackmailers could use such information for undesirable purposes that could affect personal freedom.

Some professional web sites can create files called "cookies," which identify frequent visitors. Every time you visit one of these web sites, the site knows that it's you calling again.

By tracking your on-line activities, a file could be compiled that might include your political views, your sexual orientation, what illnesses or diseases you may have suffered from, details of criminal activities in your past, and other information that many people would rather keep to themselves. A corrupt government could use information like this to manipulate the outcome of elections or eliminate "undesirable" people. Activities like this are not new, but the Internet makes it possible to collect and analyze information without the armies of secret police and informers that corrupt governments traditionally use.

FACT

A new system called WAP (Wireless Application Protocol) enables people to access the Internet through a new generation of mobile phones. It will free the Internet from the home and office, so that anyone can use it anywhere, even while on the move, just as easily as making a mobile phone call.

People are often prepared to give market research organizations very personal information about themselves when their anonymity is assured. They may mistakenly believe that on-line questionnaires that don't require them to give their names and addresses are equally anonymous. Internet connections are not anonymous. It is this mistaken belief that has enabled the police to track Internet criminals and could enable other organizations to gather information about people.

Making it simple

Most people get on-line by using a desktop or portable computer. Many people find computers off-putting because they seem to be such complicated pieces of technology. In the future, we will use simpler and more familiar devices to get on-line—"browser" telephones, mobile phone "communicators," and "interactive" television sets. Logging on will be as easy as making a phone call or switching on the television.

Twenty-first-century Internet

In the late 1990s, the value of many Internet companies rose rapidly even though many of them had never made a profit. Investors seemed to value

The chief executives of America Online and Time Warner announce the merger of their two companies.

VIEWPOINTS

"What this merger [between AOL and Time Warner] invites is the possibility of a new era in American communications that sees the end of an independent press."
Tom Rosentiel, Director of the Project for Excellence in Journalism

"This is not just about big business. This is not just about money. This is about making a better world for people."
Gerald Levin, Chairman designate, AOL Time Warner

the companies highly in the belief that they would make large profits in the future. Then, at the beginning of the year 2000, the biggest business takeover in history was announced, and it involved an Internet company. The Internet Service Provider AOL announced that it was to merge with Time Warner, the world's biggest media company, forming a business with a value of $286 billion. It was described as the Internet's coming of age. Other media and communications giants and Internet businesses are expected to start joining forces in the same way, bringing the Internet, television, and telephones together in new ways. Some people worry that these huge corporations will swallow up many of the smaller Internet companies and concentrate Internet services and web site ownership in too few hands.

The haves and have-nots

Computers and the Internet have become an essential part of business so rapidly that people who have been out of work and have not kept up with new technology could find themselves at a disadvantage when they try to return to work. People who have been unemployed for some time, or who have taken time out to bring up children, could find it difficult to get back into employment again without retraining. People who can't afford to have Internet services at home could drop farther and farther behind, while the rest of society benefits from the information, shopping, banking, communications, and entertainment services on the Internet. Could we be heading for a two-tier society of on-liners and off-liners?

More and more of us are certain to be surfing the Internet in the coming years, although we won't be doing it like this!

Divided societies are usually troubled societies. Rebelling under-classes have triggered some of the greatest revolutions in history. In future, if the Internet becomes a vital element of everyday life, education, business, and entertainment, people who are denied access to it could become an Internet under-class. Or, perhaps, the on-line world will be so much the norm that the unconventionality of being an "off-liner" could become a status symbol!

The Internet will not go away. It's here to stay. It will carry on growing, spreading, and affecting our lives in more and more different ways. The issues it raises will not go away either. Only by discussing them can we develop the business practices and establish the laws that will ensure that the Internet develops safely... for all of us.

DEBATE

Should we look forward to a future with a faster, more powerful and more widespread Internet, or should we fear our on-line future?

GLOSSARY

browser a program that enables a computer to display pages from the World Wide Web

computer nerds people, usually young men, who are engrossed in computers and computing almost to the exclusion of everything else

crash the failure of a computer program so that it ceases to operate

cyber-terrorists terrorists who use computers and on-line systems instead of guns and explosives to attack organizations, governments, military forces, etc.

download to copy information from an Internet host computer into a personal computer

e-mail electronic mail—messages sent from one computer to another electronically

hacker someone who breaks into computers to view or alter the information they contain

host a computer that supplies information to other computers linked to a network

hyperlinks words, photographs, graphics, or symbols on Web pages that can connect the computer to a different Web page

millennium bug a problem that was expected to cause computers to crash on January 1, 2000, because of the way they stored the date. However, the chaos that was expected did not occur.

modem a modulator-demodulator—a device for connecting a computer to a telephone line

search engine a digital index of web sites that can be used to locate information

server a computer system that provides programs and data to a computer network

smart card a plastic card with a computer chip embedded in it; the chip stores information, which can be read and changed. Money can be transferred from a bank account to a smart card electronically.

surf to hop from web page to web page by clicking on hypertext links

Usenet User's Network, a network of computer systems that exchange messages; the network is arranged in news groups

Web another name for the World Wide Web

web site a collection of linked web pages

World Wide Web (www) documents available on the Internet, connected by hypertext links

BOOKS TO READ

Students may find the following books useful:

101 Essential Tips–Using the Internet, Chris Lewis (technical consultant), Dorling Kindersley, 1997

the.internet, Lisa Hughes, Hodder Children's Books, 1998

The Internet–the Rough Guide, Angus J. Kennedy, Rough Guides, 1999

The ideas expressed in this book came from hundreds of web sites and many recent newspapers and magazines. The author would particularly like to acknowledge the following:

An IT and Run Job by Karen Buchanan, *Focus*, July 1999. A survey of cyber-crime

The Day the Internet Grew Up by Edward Heathcoat Amory, *Daily Mail* (London), January 12, 2000

Facing the Future, a *Newsweek* special edition, by various authors, *Newsweek*, December 1999–February 2000

Girl Power is the New Face of the Net Generation by Tony Halpin, *Daily Mail*, December 29, 1999

High Speed Internet, a special report by various authors, *Scientific American*, October 1999

How Hackers Break In, a special report by various authors, *Scientific American*, October 1998

It's a Steal by Duncan Graham-Rowe, *New Scientist*, March 4, 2000. On cyber-crime

Policing Cyberspace by Caroline Green, *Focus*, October 1998. A survey of cyber-crime

Shopping Around the Web, from *The Economist*, February 26–March 3, 2000. A survey of e-commerce

Who Wants Privacy? by Paul Wallich, *Scientific American*, April 2000

Who Wants to be Another e-millionaire? by Chris Edwards, *Focus*, June 2000

USEFUL ADDRESSES

http://www.activision.com
Internet games

http://www.aol.com
Internet Service Provider

http://www.bbc.co.uk/news
Internet-related news stories

http://www.compuserve.com
Internet Service Provider

http://www.eff.org
The Electronic Frontier Foundation, a pressure group for free speech on the Internet

http://www.epic.org
The Electronic Privacy Information Centre, a research group highlighting personal privacy and civil liberties issues relating to the Internet

http://www.excite.co.uk
Internet search engine

http://www.fbi.com
The Federal Bureau of Investigation cyber-crime details

http://www.gosci.com
The Computer Security Institute cyber-crime surveys

http://www.indexoncensorship.org
Index on Censorship, a pressure group for free expression

http://www.infoworld.com
Internet-related news stories

http://www.lycos.co.uk
Internet search engine

http://www.microsoft.com/games
Internet games

http://www.msn.com
Internet Service Provider

http://www.newscientist.com
Internet-related articles and news

http://www.nop.co.uk
National Opinion Polls' Internet survey results

http://www.peacefire.org
Peacefire, a pressure group for free speech on the Internet

http://www.sciam.com
Internet-related articles and news

http://www.sony.com
Entertainment

http://www.yahoo.co.uk
Internet search engine

INDEX

Number in **bold** refer to illustrations.

Amazon 40, 53
America Online 58, **58**

back doors 39
Barnes and Noble 54
blocking programs 5
British Library 28
browsers 22

card number generators 42–43
Central Intelligence Agency (CIA) 40
CERN 6, **6**, 7
chat rooms 24, 48
Clinton, Bill **41**
computer nerds 17
copyright 41–42
cyber attacks 40
cyberchondriacs 14–15
cyber-crime 38, 50, 51
cyberspace 4, 6, 20, 34
cyber-stalking 48, **48**,
cyber-terrorists 49, 50, 51

digital photographs 16, **16**, 17

e-business 32–37, **32**, 52
e-mail **7**, 8, 10–12, **10**, 16, **16**, 18, 23, 24, 26, 32, 44, 45, 46, 47, 48, 50, 55

Federal Bureau of Investigation (FBI) **40**, 44, 48, **50**
"following the Sun" 36
fraud 42–44
freedom of information 18–23, 45

Gates, Bill 22
Gibson, William 6
Gore, Al 5

hackers 38, 39, **39**, 40, **40**
hosts 11
hyperlinks 6

information superhighway 4–5
International Chamber of Commerce 51
Internet
- access 21, 23
- addiction 30
- cafés **12**, 18
- and censorship 4, 19, **19**, 30, 45
- and children 17, **17**, 24–31
- and crime 4, 38–51
- and developing world 21, 34
- and design 32–33, **33**
- and education 26–27, **26**
- invention of 4
- and pornography 30
- and privacy 4
- and senior citizens 13, **13**
- and sexually explicit material 44–45
- and women 12–13, **12**, 34

Internet Service Providers (ISPs) 10–11, 13, 17, 25, 45, 58
intranet 36

Microsoft 22, **22**, 54
mobile phones 7, 21, 54, 57

National Criminal Intelligence Service (NCIS) 51
National Portrait Gallery 28

news groups 25
NHS Direct 15

on-line
 art galleries 28–29, **28**
 banking 8, 13
 books 53–54
 elections 22–23
 games 25, **25**, 26
 interpreters 20
 machines 54–55, **54**
 medical advice 14, **14**, 16
 museums 28–29, **28**
 share-dealing 36–37, **37**, 43–44
 shopping 6, 8, **8**, 9, **9**, 10, 13, **43**
 stock market trading 36–37, 43–44
 video links 16

passwords 39, 40
pedophile activities 51, **51**
Pentagon 50

routers 40

search engines 14, 40
servers 40
smart cards 55, **55**
Smith, David **47**
software piracy 42
surfers 23, **25**, 28–29, 40, **59**

Tenenbaum, Ehud **40**
Time Warner 58, **58**

U.S. Software Publishers Association 42
Usenet 25

video-conferencing 12
virtual business 35
virtual graveyards 16
virtual reality 6
viruses 46–47, 50
 "Lovebug, the" 47
 "Melissa" 46, 47, **47**
webcams 12, 15, 16
webmail 11
web sites 6, 9, 11, 13, 14 , 15, 16, 17, 18, 19, 20, 27, 28, 29, 30, 31, 32, 33, 35, 40, 42, 44, 45, 49, 50, 53, 54, 55, 58
Wireless Application Protocol (WAP) 57
World Wide Web 6, **6**, 7, 8, 9, 14, 15, 16, 17, 19, 21, 23, 25, 29, 30, 33, 53

Yahoo 40